The stupidly simple guide to s..._ ....._..._ _ .

THIS IS DEDICATED TO MY LATE GRANDMOTHER.

ABOUT THE AUTHOR

MIVIAN HEGARTY WAS BORN AND RAISED IN IRELAND. SHE IS A REIKI MASTER TEACHER AND HAS A KEEN INTEREST IN SPIRITUALITY, SELF HELP, PERSONAL GROWTH, WRITING, AND MUSIC.

INTRODUCTION

As I am a keen writer, I write absolutely everything down. I absolutely love a pen and paper to write everything down. I do lists on a daily, weekly, and monthly basis.

I like to set myself goals and it gives me great pleasure when I achieve them.

If I don't get to something I do not beat myself up, which would defeat the purpose of the exercise. Sometimes unexpected things can arise and that's ok. As soon as I can I get myself back on track. If I don't do it, no one else will.

I wrote this book, in the hope it may help other people gain clarity, with getting their lives back on track. Whilst I don't claim to be an expert, I have used this strategy in my own life.

Chapter Seven   A work in progress.

Life Lessons

When we were children, my late Grandmother always told us to "Live each day as if it's your last and one day you will be right." I have found it to be a great way of keeping perspective on things. Every day I think of these words and I have found them to be motivational when I need to kick myself into gear. When you sit down and think about it if it truly was your last day, how and with whom would you want to spend it? As soon as I answer it, I learn about my priorities. Would you want to waste it or would you want to spend it in the pursuit of getting your act together and making the most of your time here? This is the question I have come back to time and time again, in my life if I experience doubts. I have applied them to jobs, relationships, friendships, etc.,

When we were children we sometimes would moan at having to go out if the weather was bad, to which my Mother would remind us that people were dying in hospital who would never get the opportunity to go outside again. They would not care what the weather was like if they were given the opportunity to go outside again. She was absolutely right. If you are lucky enough to have the opportunity to go out into the world and start over, you are indeed very lucky. Never take that for granted.

It is never too late to start over. Every day is a new beginning, with endless possibilities.

"Do not squander time for that is the stuff life is made of"

Benjamin Franklin

CHAPTER ONE
CONGRATULATIONS

So, you were born, well lucky you?! Despite the odds, you, yes you were the one that "made the grade" and here you are, you beautiful miracle. You made it, congratulations. You are unique, a one of a kind never to be repeated. Think about that for a minute. I mean really think about that. You are the one that was born and despite hardships, you may have faced in life, you are still alive.

How would you like to use the time, you have been given? My mother always told us there are certain things you cannot buy, no matter how much money you have. Time is one of those things and when you look back on your life, do you want to feel that you have "wasted" it, or would you prefer to feel like you got your act together and actually used your time here wisely?

The choice is ultimately of course yours.

It's never too late to start over.

It is a privilege to be alive. Treat it as such and make the most of it. Look, I am not saying that I haven't had moments myself where I am having a bad day, but I find reminding myself that I am here at all to be such a great way of not taking things for granted.

None of us know how much time we have so let's make the most of it. The fact that you are reading this means you clearly want to make some changes. If you want to continue as you are, then knock yourself out. But, if you truly want to make a change, re-member as I said, it is never too late.

Get up and show up, this is your Life!

This is your opportunity to make the absolute best of it. As far as I am aware this is the only life we get.

So "carpe diem."

We have no time to waste.

CHAPTER TWO

Questions to ask yourself.

When I want to make changes in my life, there are some questions I ask myself. It means being really honest with myself. I prefer to write down the answers, and then I read them back to myself out loud. That way I gain clarity.

Am I happy with how I am living my life?

Do I feel I am living the life I actually want?

If not what am I doing to change it?

What exactly do I do every day?

If it was my last day on Earth, would I be happy with how I am spending it?

I will show you later a good way of clarifying what you do with your time if you are unsure. This is my no-nonsense way of highlighting where and how you spend your time. So, you won't be able to use the excuse, "But, I don't have the time." I am going to blow that excuse out of the water.

What would I like to do?

How am I going to achieve that?

Now, I am not saying you won't fall flat on your face, in life. I have lost count of the number of times I have fallen flat on my face. But, you know what I far prefer to live life being a risk-taker and taking chances than playing it safe. Some of the best lessons I have learned have come from mistakes. If something works, fantastic. If it doesn't then start over or try something else. You may be better equipped the next time around with some of the invaluable lessons you have learned. In saying that I am not advising that you throw caution to the wind and stride into work in the morning and hand your notice in unless you have the means to survive.

CHAPTER THREE
TIME AUDIT

If you feel you have no time, well like I said earlier I am going to show you how you free some time up.

What I have found useful for myself is to write down just exactly how I am using my time. In the next chapter, you will find some blank time audit pages. It can be extremely useful for time management, if you don't know how you are using your time or what you are spending it doing, you will find it tough to make changes. I am brutally honest with myself and I write down everything and yes I mean absolutely everything I do on a daily basis. If you do this, you will probably begin to see patterns emerging, that perhaps you weren't aware of. It can be a real eye-opener.

If you stick with it, you may be able to see where you are spending your time and claw some time back.

Remember, be completely honest with yourself! If you really want to changes things, it is up to you.

 I have left the pages completely blank for you to fill in the day and time yourself. I was going to use a template, but then I said I would let you take the responsibility for working out your own strategy for how you want to complete it. Do it over a week, eg. Television, Social Media, Work, Sleep, etc.,

Don't total everything off until the end.

TIME AUDIT

I want you to add up and total where you are spending your time and I mean for everything. That includes television, social media, etc.,

You may be surprised at some of the totals you have.

Use the pages I have left blank to total everything off.

Include everything work, sleep, television, social media, household chores...

TOTALS PAGE.

Do you still think you have no time?

So, now I want you to start looking at where you can claw time back. This is where you start to cull inefficient time-wasting.

Can you get up 30 minutes earlier, to focus on something you really want to do? Doing this seven days a week gives you 3.5 hours. Those lie-ons at the weekend do not seem so harmless now, do they?

If you give something up eg. Watching Television how much time will you claw back? Cut back by even 30 minutes seven days a week and that is another 3.5 hours a week.

That's already seven hours a week.

It's really up to you, how ruthlessly you want to go through your schedule. Either you are serious about changing your life, or you are not. It is important to be realistic though and allow time for self-care.

It's really a tool to work out if a task is absolutely essential and what you can do to get time back. Everyone has activities that are essential to life e.g. work, childcare, sleep, etc.,

The ones to focus on are the activities that are not essential e.g Social Media, watching Television.

It is important that you do spend time on a hobby or just something that makes you feel good. But, just get rid of, or curtail some of the non -essential things. That will free up time, to focus on something you want to achieve.

CHAPTER FOUR

WHAT DO YOU WANT TO DO?

Ok, so now that you have clawed back time.

You want to work out what you want to spend your time doing. If you are unsure of what you want to do with your life and feel that you are wasting it. Here are some questions I find helpful to ask.

What talents do I have?

What are my values?

What am I really passionate about?

What am I really good at, something that comes really easily to you?

Is there anything that I would like to do, but you just never had the time?

If you were given the chance what would you willingly do for free, on a daily basis if you had the chance? What sets your soul on fire?

Hopefully, you can get a few ideas down on paper. I have left the next page blank so you can jot down a few ideas. I find it helpful to write a few ideas down.

IDEAS PAGE

GET SCRIBBLING!

CHAPTER FIVE

DEVELOP A PLAN

Remember, a ship does not reach its destination without charting its course.

"If you fail to plan, you are planning to fail."

If you have come up with some ideas of what you would like to do, then you will need some kind of plan to work towards that.

e.g I will study a college course, so I can change careers. Get specific on what it is you want to do.

What can you do to work towards that? Do you need to research college courses?

Create a daily routine. If you really want to change your life, you will need a routine that you can put in place and stick to it.

KPI's or Key performance indicators are a tool used in business as a way of measuring how a company is achieving its business objectives. Again you can apply this to your life. It can keep you motivated towards your goals.

Most people are also very familiar with the SMART principle, in the workplace.

Specific; Your goals are clearly defined.

Measurable; You need to be able to measure your goals.

Attainable; Choose something that is attainable.

Relevant; Is this goal relevant to the life you want for yourself?

Timed; Set yourself a timeframe to achieve it.

Again, I am stressing the importance of setting achievable goals. If you set yourself unattainable targets and you fail to meet all of them, you run the risk of having the opposite of your desired effect. Take for example you want to get up 1 hour earlier, in the morning. To begin with, you can get up 15 minutes earlier, for a week and the second week get up 30 minutes earlier. Take bite-sized chunks out of it and prioritize just a few goals e.g study or career change. Perhaps you want to change your career and you are going to enroll in a college course, to pursue that. I have left the next page blank for you to put down on paper what exactly you are going to do and the following is for your routine.

Again, they are both blank pages so you can come up with your own plan. I have found the more invested in the process I am, the more likely I am to stick to the routine.

MY GOALS

MY ROUTINE

You can always get an accountability partner if you are still struggling. You can keep each other in check. It is also helpful to take some time each day to reflect on what you have achieved and if you are still on track. Just a few minutes is all you need to reflect. Don't beat yourself up, if you didn't achieve what you set out to do. If you "fall off the wagon", get back on it and start again.

Finding a mentor can also be extremely helpful if you want to achieve something. Finding someone you aspire to be, is a fantastic way of gaining knowledge from someone who has a wealth of experience, whether it be in business or even personal development.

CHAPTER SIX.

A WORK IN PROGRESS.

By now, hopefully, you have a clearer plan of what your goals are and have made plans to achieve them. Remember, take action and also remember you are a work in progress.

Make sure to celebrate your achievements. No matter how small. You are making progress and that is something to celebrate. When you acknowledge your achievements, it can motivate you to achieve more.

The bottom line is the only person who can change you is you.

Get up and show up this is your life.

Nobody else is going to do it for you.

You can do this.

Have faith in yourself.

If you are still having problems, getting motivated you may need to look at getting some professional help i.e Counselling, as to why that is.

DISCLAIMER

This book contains general advice and information only. It should not be used to replace the advice of your doctor or another trained health professional. If you think you have a health problem, it is recommended that you seek your physician's advice before embarking on any program. Please consult with your physician before undertaking any fitness regime or dietary change. The publisher and author disclaim liability for any medical outcomes that may occur as a result of applying the methods contained in this book. The author does not claim to be an expert in this field. The purpose of this book is to provide general information and advice only.

by Mivian Hegarty

.

Printed in Great Britain
by Amazon

78431151R00020